from UNINCORPORATED TERRITORY

[lukao]

Previous Works

from unincorporated territory [hacha]
(Tinfish Press, 2008; reprinted by Omnidawn Publishing, 2017)

from unincorporated territory [saina]
(Omnidawn Publishing, 2010)

from unincorporated territory [guma']
(Omnidawn Publishing, 2014)

from UNINCORPORATED TERRITORY

[lukao]

CRAIG SANTOS PEREZ

OMNIDAWN PUBLISHING
OAKLAND, CALIFORNIA
2017

Cover art:
Photograph by Jack Gray, "The Matao New Performance Project at Lasso' Fuha developing Fanhasso, a contemporary dance directed by Dåkot-ta Alcantara-Camacho at the Festival of Pacific Arts 2016"

Photograph by Craig Santos Perez, "Kaikainali'i at the Waikīkī Aquarium"

"poemaps" (poem-maps) designed by Craig Santos Perez & Donovan Kūhiō Colleps;
created by Donovan Kūhiō Colleps.

Cover typeface: Palatino LT Std & Perpetua Std
Interior typefaces: Adobe Garamond Pro

Cover & Interior layout by Cassandra Smith
Design by Craig Santos Perez

Offset printed in the United States
by Edwards Brothers Malloy, Ann Arbor, Michigan
On 55# Glatfelter B18 Antique
Acid Free Archival Quality Recycled Paper

Library of Congress Cataloging-in-Publication Data

Names: Santos Perez, Craig, author.
Title: From unincorporated territory [lukao] / Craig Santos Perez.
Description: Richmond, California : Omnidawn Publishing, 2017.
Identifiers: LCCN 2017020704 | ISBN 9781632430410
(paperback : alk. paper)
Classification: LCC PS3619.A598 A6 2017 | DDC 811/.6--dc23
LC record available at https://lccn.loc.gov/2017020704

Published by Omnidawn Publishing, Oakland, California
www.omnidawn.com (510) 237-5472 (800) 792-4957
10 9 8 7 6 5 4 3 2 1
ISBN: 978-1-63243-041-0

Map of Contents

~

hånom håga' hånom

~

~

~

~

“Everyday is a reenactment of the creation story.”

—Joy Harjo *from* “A Postcolonial Tale”

~

dedicated to my wife, Brandy Nālani, addressed as "[you]"
and to my daughter, Kaikainali'i, addressed as "[neni]"

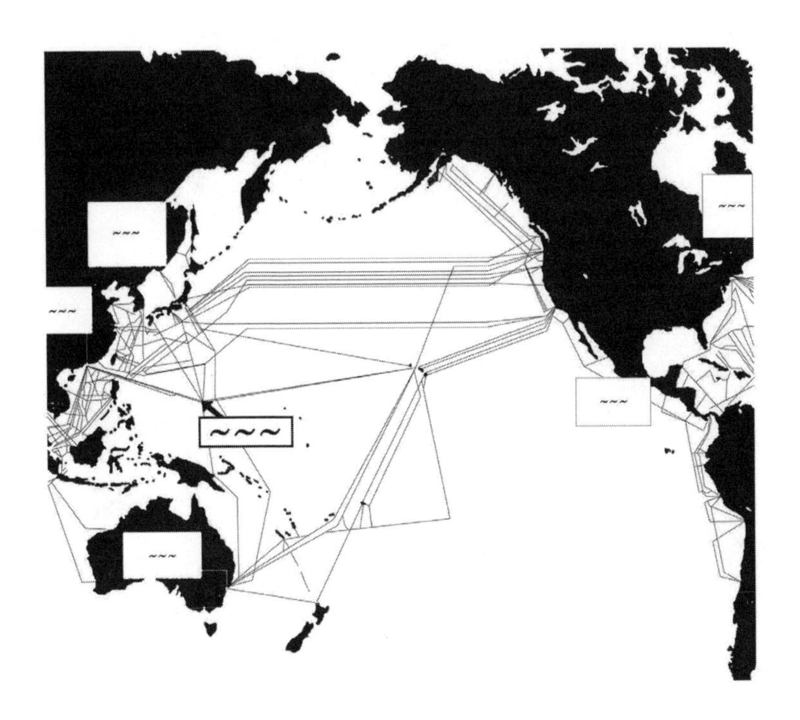

poemap based on "Telegeography cable network map, 2009," from "Critical Nodes, Cultural Networks: Re-Mapping Guam's Cable Infrastructure," by Nicole Starosielski in *Amerasia Journal* 37:3 (2011): 18-27.

"Undersea communication cables are durable and cost-effective infrastructures supporting the interconnection of America, Asia, and Australia. Many of these cables, which carry almost all transpacific Internet traffic, are routed through the island of Guam. Historically, more cables have landed on Guam than in either Hawai'i or California, two other major hubs for signal exchange." (19)

because america

from **the legends of juan malo** *(a malologue)*

~

(the birth of Guam)

Guam was born on March 6, 1521, when Ferdinand Magellan arrived in the womb of Humåtak Bay and delivered [us] into the calloused hands of modernity. "Guam is Where Western Imperialism in the Pacific Begins!" St. Helena Augusta, tayuyute [ham] : *pray for [us]*. The annual reenactment of "Discovery Day" is a must see for all tourists: Chamorros-dressed-as-our-ancestors welcome Chamorros-dressed-as-the-galleon-crew. After the bloody performance, enjoy local food, walking tours, live reggae bands, and fireworks! Guam was adopted on December 10, 1898, when the Treaty of Paris was signed, and Spain ceded [us] to the United States. "Guam is Where America's Western Frontier Begins!" Guam was declared an "unincorporated territory" on May 27, 1901, when the Supreme Court Insular Cases decided that the U.S. constitution does not follow its flag. "Guam is Where America's Logic of Territorial Incorporation Ends!" Guam was kidnapped on December 8, 1941, when Japan bombed, invaded, and occupied [us]. "Guam is Where the Greater East Asia Co-Prosperity Sphere Begins!" On July 21, 1944, the U.S. armed forces returned and defeated the Japanese military. Guam was naturalized on August 1, 1950, when the Organic Act bestowed U.S. citizenship upon [us]. "Guam is Where America's Passports Begin!" Guam was pimped out on May 1, 1967, when Pan American World Airways arrived with the first 109 Japanese tourists. The Guam Visitors Bureau birthed a new marketing slogan: "Guam is Where America's Day Begins!" Since Guam is located 2,000 miles west of the international dateline, [we] instagram the sunrise before anyone in the fifty states. For the past 30 years, a straw poll on Guam has accurately predicted U.S. presidential elections, even though our votes don't actually count in the electoral college. "Guam is Where America's Voting Rights End!" This ironic streak ended in 2016, when Hillary Clinton received 70% of the ballots cast on Guam, yet Donald Trump still won #notmycolonizerinchief. St. Thomas More, tayuyute [ham]. After the election, [we] begin the countdown to *Super Bowl Monday*, a sacred day when all Chamorros leave work and school in procession to the altar of the television. St. Sebastian, tayuyute [ham]. I attended George Washington High School on Guam, but I often skipped "English" class because the haole teacher made [us] memorize boring, canonical verse. "Guam is Where America's Poetry Begins!" Sorry not sorry if I threw everyone's rhyme and meter off.

ginen **understory**

~

(first trimester)

[we] are watching a documentary
about home birth when [you] first feel

[neni] kick // if our doctor recommends
a "c-section" \\ if [we] cut open

the bellies of whales and birds,
what fragments will [we] shore //

plastic multiplies, leaches toxins, litters
the beaches of o'ahu : *this gathering*

place, this embryo \\ plastic is the "perfect"
creation because it never dies // i wish

our daughter was derived
from oil so that she will survive

our wasteful hands // so that
she, too, will have a "great future"

(pō)

~

before i first visit [you]
in ka'a'awa // before
[we] swim in salt water
and forage the tide
for shells \\ before [we]
learn our body
languages // before i
mistake trade winds
for your hair \\
before [we] dive
// before [we] come
against wreckage \\
before [we] close
our eyes to see
what night asks [us]
to let go // before
the emotional
chickens crow the sun
risen \\ before vow
-els and consonants //
before was pō \\
the first darkness
birthing our sea
of moving islands

(i tinituhon)

~

wheredoislands
beginandendspiral
timewavecon-
tractions30
minutesapart
alphabetsare
constellationsofbone
hookssounding
linesamnioticfluidis
90%hånom:*water*
"hacha"originarrival
should[we]go
tothehospital
lukao:*procession*

(dear fu'una)

~

first nana : *mother*,
this is my first prayer
to you, full of
wonder // taotao
manu hao : *where
are you from* \\
what made you leave
your first guma' : *home* //
so many of [us] have left
guåhan
for military and school,
jobs and hospitals \\
forgive me, i lost
our fino' haya : *first
language* in transit, ghost
words // who'll translate
me to you \\ i clutched
my passport aboard
i batkon aire : *the air
boat* to san francisco //
what did you carry
aboard i sakman :
the outrigger canoe \\
how did you let

(first ocean)
during the rim of the pacific military exercises, 2014

~

when [neni] was newborn, [you] rinsed
her in the sink // pilot whales, deafened

by sonar, are bloated and stranded
ashore \\ now [you] bathe her in the tub,

clean behind her ears, sing "my island
maui," written by your dad // his ashes

scattered in the pacific decades ago
\\ when [we] bring [neni] to the beach

for the first time, [you] secure her
to your chest and walk into the sea \\

what will the aircrafts, ships, soldiers,
and weapons of 22 nations take from [us]

// "i wish she could've met my dad," [you] say \\
schools of recently spawned fish, lifeless,

spoil the tidelands // is oceania memorial
or target, economic zone or monument,

territory or mākua // a cold salt wind surges
\\ [we] shiver like generations of coral reef

bleaching

ginen **organic acts**

Our entrance to the past is through memory—either oral or written. And water. In this case salt water. Sea water. And, as the ocean appears to be the same yet is constantly in motion, affected by tidal movements, so too this memory appears stationary yet is shifting always. Repetition drives the event and the memory simultaneously, becoming a haunting, becoming spectral in its nature.

—M. NourbeSe Philip *from ZONG*

~

fairfield, california, circa 2008 // grandma lights votive candles, dusts the wooden crucifix, and kisses her lisayu : *rosary : procession of prayers* \\ then [we] sit on the couch and she begins her daily recitation : "gi na'ån i tata i lahi-na yan i espiritu sånto åmen

gi tinituhon : *in the beginning* fu'una transforms her brother puntan's back into tano' : *land*, chest into langet : *sky*, eyes into atdao : *sun* and pulan : *moon* // then her breath blooms the odda' : *soil* and acho' tasi : *coral* \\ then she dives into the place [we] will name humåtak bay // then her body calcifies into the stone from which [we] were born \\ laso fu'a : *creation point*

grandma prays : "umatuna i tata i lahi-na yan i espiritu sånto taiguihi i tutuhom-na yan pågo yan siempre yan i minaihinekkok na ha'åne åmen

~

as a patgon : *child*, i never heard the creation story of our first mother, fu'una (whose name translates as *first*), or our first *father*, puntan (whose name translates as *coconut sapling*) //
grandma always said "in the beginning was the word and the word was god

her fingers erode
rosary beads // waves erode
coasts \\ words erode
silence

[we] pray : "manhongge yo' as yu'us tåta ni todu ha' hana'sina na hana'huyong i langet yan i tano'

~

in the past, our ancestors pilgrimaged each year to laso fu'a // they made offerings and asked blessings for *simiya* : seed, hale' : *root*, and talaya : *net* \\ they stood in circles and chanted rhymed verses back and forth // [we] call this communal poetic form kåntan chamorrita (which translates as *to sing both forwards and backwards*)

"manhihigai hit pa'go" : *[we] are thatching now*
"para ta afte in gima'-ta"
"para i leheng-ta para u fa'maolek"
"para todu i familia-ta"

ginen **Ka Lāhui o ka Pō Interview**

September 27, 2014

~

[you]: I was in labor for 24 hours. The contractions were easy at first, but they grew intense in the transition phase. It felt like I was in another place and time didn't exist in the same way as it did before.

Helen: I gave birth to Brian in 1975, when I was 23 years old. We were living in Toto, Guam, in a small wooden house that your dad built. My doctor was from the Seventh Day Adventist Clinic. His wife was my midwife. They believed in natural childbirth. Everyday I did sit-ups and leg stretches and walking. One night we went to a party and we danced and ate pizza. Though I could only slow dance because I was close to my due date.

[you]: We weren't sure if we were going to go to the hospital or do a home birth. After six hours of labor in transition, our midwife said : "We're at that point where you have to decide."

Helen: When we got home, I felt bloated, full. I took a shower and then my water broke. We went to Guam Memorial Hospital. I was dilated 4 centimeters. They said to walk the hallways. So I was walking, walking, walking.

[you]: From the beginning I knew I wanted to have a natural childbirth, so I wanted to have the baby at home. Once I started pushing I felt like all the intense contractions gave me strength. The pushing took only a half hour. Then she was born.

Helen: I took lamaze class. In the class they told us to bring a picture to focus on. I loved taking pictures of the beach, especially Ritidian.* I kept breathing and looking at the picture. Your dad was massaging me and giving me ice. The whole time I was praying.

[you]: She opened her eyes immediately. Craig got to see her first. When she came out, she looked surprised. She looked at me and seemed to say "Oh, that's what you look like, Mommy." Craig put her on me, and she was crying, but then she immediately settled down when I held her.

Helen: Brian was born in the morning, and I could feel the fluids come out of me. They washed him and brought him to me and the nurse showed me how to breastfeed. I only tore a little bit. Then your dad cut the cord. Later they swaddled Brian real tight and took our picture.

Tom: I remember the maternity ward was next to the mental ward. You could hear screaming. So I slept on the chair beside your mom all night because I wanted to protect her.

~~In Chamorro birthing practices, a pattera (midwife) and a surahåna (healer) guided the pregnant mother. They offered åmot (medicine) and lasa (massage). Family provided food, such as fresh chicken soup and eggs. Most families paid in meat and produce from their farms. After delivery, the baby was cleaned and massaged with coconut oil. The apuya' (umbilical cord) and påres (placenta) were buried beneath or near the house because Chamorros believe that doing so would keep children close to home throughout their lives.~~

ginen island of no birdsong

"It was the heavy silence. A dawn in the tropics without bird sounds bordered on the surreal. The silence was so complete that it seemed to be audible, and so eerie that I felt like shuddering.

There were no more native forest birds in southern Guam. Their last stand was in the northern third of the island. Rachel Carson's silent spring was already a year-round affair in southern Guam.

Extinction was no longer some textbook abstraction here; it was a reality—a silent reality."

—L. C. Shelton *from* "Captive Propagation of the Micronesian Kingfisher" (1986)

~

"day one : blind and naked"

fanhasso : *remember* studying native birds of guam in school // "the micronesian kingfisher, or sihek, can see into the water" \\ "added to the endangered species list in 1984" // "the last wild birds were captured and transferred to american zoos for captive breeding" \\ vocabulary test : "invasive, colonize, extirpate, extinct" // 44,000 chamorros now live in california \\ 15,000 in washington // what does not change \\ st gail, tayuyute [ham] : *pray for [us]*

~

"day two : casts produced"

"In 2010, a mated pair of Micronesian kingfishers…laid two fertile eggs this spring inside a hollowed-out palm log in a special breeding room of the Chicago Lincoln Park Zoo bird house. Keepers promptly stole one of the eggs…The parents incubated and hatched one egg in the hollow log…The other egg hatched a few days later inside an incubation machine in a lab, where the chick now lives, fed by keepers from tweezers protruding beneath the beak of an oversized kingfisher hand puppet

"violent care"

~

"day five : flight feather tracts visible on wings"

""hu hongge i lina'la'
tataotao ta'lo åmen""
i want to believe in
the resurrection of
our bodies
because i have no
memories of bird

-song
"kshh-skshh-skshh-kroo-ee kroo-ee kroo-ee

#prayfor________
#prayfor________
#prayfor________
#prayfor________
#prayfor________
#prayfor________
#prayfor________
#prayfor________
#prayfor________
#prayfor________

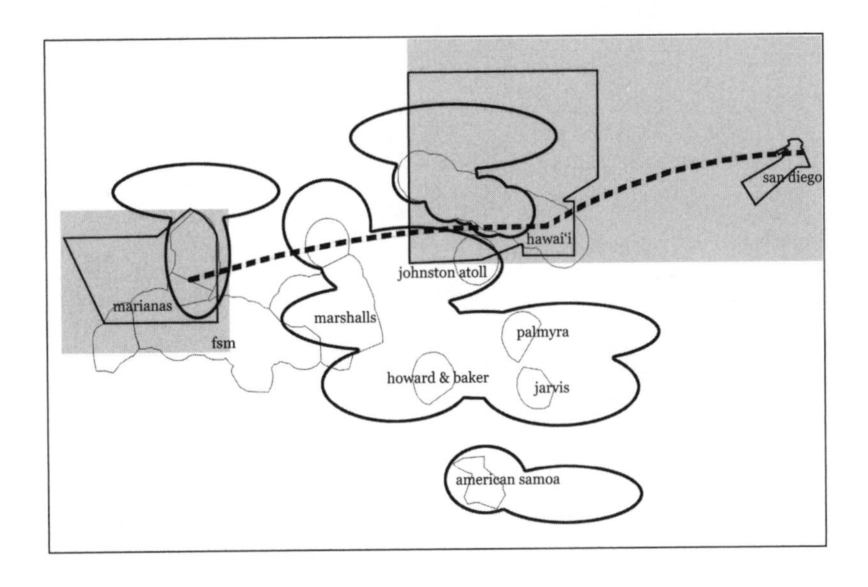

poemap based on the "Key US Bases in Pacific Pivot Buildup" map, prepared by Juan Wilson of Island Breath (www.islandbreath.org) (30 July 2014, Revision: 1.3.1). Sources: Map A: Mariana Island Training Area EIS (http://mitt-eis.com/), Map B: NOAA IOOS: Pacific Ocean States, territories, etc (http://www.ioos.noaa/gov/regions/pacioos.html), and Map C: DITC: Acoustic Effects on Marine Mammals (http://dtic.mil/dtic/tr/fulltext/u2/a560973.pdf) Page 3.

can't demilitarize

from **the legends of juan malo** (a malologue)

~

(the birth of Guåhan)

"Guam" is now named "Guåhan," which translates as *[we] have*. As in *[we] have* deep water and the U.S. expects [us] to home port 60% of the Pacific fleet. Or *[we] have* to continue supporting the Navy (one team, no seams). Or *[we] have* a last place ranking in annual per capita medical spending on Chamorro veterans #islandofforgottenwarriors. St Michael the Archangel, tayuyute [ham]. "Guam" is now named "Guåhan," which translates as *[we] have*. As in *[we] have* resources for the taking. Or *[we] have* our customers' needs as our first priority. Or *[we] have* to change our name after the Obama administration referred to the East Wing of the White House as "Guam, pleasant but powerless." "Guam" is now named "Guåhan," which translates as *[we] have*. As in *[we] have* many nicknames, including USS Guam, The Tip of America's Spear, Unsinkable Aircraft Carrier, Superfortress Guam, The Trailer Park of the Pacific, America's Gateway to Asia, and Micronesia's Gateway to America. "Guam" is now named "Guåhan," which translates as *[we] have*. As in *[we] have* been tricked out and targeted. Or *[we] have* tourism 2020 vision when setting forth a plan for the future. Or *[we] have* a charmingly exotic, endangered look. "Guam" is now named "Guåhan," which translates as *[we] have*. As in *[we] have* to change our name after Mariah Carey appeared on American talk shows with a dog she got in Mexico and named "Guam" : "Here Guam, here Guam, stop hiding Guam, Guam is a good boy." St. Roch, tayuyute [ham]. "Guam" is now named "Guåhan," which translates as *[we] have*. As in *[we] have* many names for our people, including Chamorro, Chamoru, Tsamoru, CHamoru, Guamese, Guamesian, Guamish, Guamaniac, Guamanian, Guatemalan, Chaud, Indios, Mestizo, and Mexican. "Guam" is now named "Guåhan," which translates as *[we] have*. As in *[we] have* serious identity issues because our original meaning has been translated as "lost."

ginen **understory**

~

(second trimester)

[you] and i walk to our community garden
plot in mānoa // when do they douse glyphosate

along sidewalks \\ genetically modified crops
are developed in hawai'i because the tropics

yield 3 times annually // syngenta, dow,
monsanto \\ how will open air pesticide drift

affect our unborn daughter, whose nerve
endings are just beginning to root // the organic

seed packets in my pocket sound like a toy rattle \\
do profits from cattle feed, ethanol, and corn syrup

justify evacuating our schools when they spray
nearby fields // does growing their "perfect" seed

justify our birth defects \\ [we] dig and plant,
dirt under fingernails // what will our children

be able to harvest in this paradise of fugitive
d

u

s

t

(maui)

~

baits
his bone hook
with wings //
raises the sea
        -bed \\ i propose
to [you] atop haleakalā
at sunrise, cliché //
hundreds of tourists
taking the same picture
\\ a year later, in huelo,
maui, [we] recite our vows
at sunset // cast
flowers over the cliff,
and into the ocean,
for your dad

(i tinituhon)

~

light dilates

mānoa valley and

the ko‘olau mountains

where do islands

end and begin

time spiraling fractions

10 minutes apart

departure destination

swell forecast

“hugua”

eggs boil

sounding lines

measure distances

between stars

lukao

(dear puntan)

~

first tata : *father*
this is my first prayer
to you, full of questions //
what was your father's name
\\ where is he buried //
        what song maps
did he teach you
before crossing ocean
// when you planted
the first coconut sapling
here, when its roots pushed
through husk into soil,
did you feel belonging \\
        you sacrificed
your known world
so that [we] will inherit
shelter // is this
what it means to be
a father

(first teeth)

~

[neni] cries from teething // how do parents
comfort a kid in pain, bullied in school, shot

by a power drunk cop #justiceforkollinelderts
\\ [you] gently massage her gums with your

fingers // count how many children killed in gaza
this hour of siege \\ how do [we] wipe away tear

-gas and blood, provide shelter from snipers,
disarm occupying armies #freepalestine //

[you] recite the hawaiian alphabet song
to [neni] \\ what lullabies echo inside detention

centers and traverse teething borders to soothe
thousands of youth atop la bestia #unaccompanied //

[you] rub her back warm with coconut oil
\\ how do [we] hold violence at arm's length

when raising our hands up is no longer
a sign of surrender #blacklivesmatter //

[neni] falls asleep in your cradling arms,
skin to skin, against the news \\ how will [we]

teach her to safely cross any body of water
by believing in her own breath #

ginen **organic acts**

~

grandma says :
"my mom, your great-grandma"
"called us home everyday at sunset"
"to say rosary in front of the madonna"
"she was very devoted"

the spanish brought their god and bible, suppressed the story
of fu'una and puntan, and forbade the procession
to laso fu'a in humåtak bay

"[we] were at home when the sirens came"
"the japanese are invading, everyone screamed"
"i was afraid to die" (choke point, 1941)

"during the war, neighbors come to our house"
"my mom would translate the radio voice"
"the radio was buried during the day"

~

our ancestors once buried the dead beneath the guma' latte' :
raised stone house so that their spirits would continue to dwell
close and protect [us] // even our bones are 20% hånom : *water*

~

"my mom makes a huge pot of soup"
"but [we] had to be very quiet"
"soldiers wait in the dark"

"some neighbors i never saw again"

i bury her
seeded words
in my notebook // breaking
the line when she
breathes \\ breaking the stanza

when she pauses // breaking
the page when she closes
her eyes

"every night [we] said novena"
"praying really helped during the war"
"i still carry my mom's voice with me"
"i carry it for the sake of [us]"

~

i taotaomo'na : *the spirits of before* also dwell within the space of i trunkun nunu : *the giant banyan tree*, whose aerial roots fall from branches, intertwine, fuse, and root // as time passes, new trunks form until a single tree becomes an archipelago

~

"manhihigai hit pa'go"
the alarm rings
"para ta afte in gima'-ta" : *to put a roof over our home*
grandma opens her pill organizer
"para i leheng-ta para u fa'maolek"
i bring her hånom
"para todu i familia-ta

ginen **Ka Lāhui o ka Pō Interview**

September 27, 2014

~

[me]: She was a few days late so we were on edge. Our friend Joy had an art show, and all our friends there were talking to Brandy's stomach saying, "Come out."

[you]: I actually had a contraction at the art show. Our doula, Grace, was at the show and I told her I just felt a lot of pressure. At home, I told Craig it was time.

Helen: We lost our house in Toto when a typhoon hit. We decided to move to California after that, and I wanted to go to court reporting school. I stayed at home during the day to watch Brian, and I went to school at night. I got pregnant with you in California, but I didn't want to give birth to you there. I wanted you to be born on Guam, like your brother. And I trusted my doctor and his wife.

[me]: That night the labor started. We had downloaded a hypno-birthing app that we listened to. It's basically a hippy haole trying to hypnotize you. It drove me crazy.

[you]: It helped to put me to sleep with its mantras like "Listen to your baby" and "You're opening up like a flower." That night I started timing the contractions.

Helen: I wanted you to be born in a unique place. I remember when I was going to school, whenever I told my teachers and classmates that my mom was born in Guam, everyone was interested. It was exotic to them. So we moved back to Guam.

[me]: The contractions continued through the morning. Our midwife and doula came at noon. I felt stressed because I had made food for her due date, but since she was late, we had eaten all the food. She was in labor for hours and hours, but the midwife said it would still be awhile. It was hard not knowing when it would end.

Helen: I was working at home, transcribing court documents. One afternoon, I started feeling weird. You were kicking and moving, and I started to feel nauseous. The contractions started at night, so we went to the Guam Memorial Hospital again.

[you]: There was one point, I think I had been in transition for 8 hours, I turned to Craig and said, "I don't know how much longer I can handle this."

Helen: They told me to walk up and down the halls. My water bag broke when they examined me. You were born at night, no complications. I nursed you right away and we went home the next day.

Tom: The labor was short. I kept giving your mom ice. After you were born, I cut the cord.

~~In 1907, the U.S. Navy medical officers started to regulate, certify, and license Chamorro midwives. Public law also determined midwife fees and wages: in 1925, $2.50 to $10.00 per patient; in 1936, a $10.00 minimum fee; in 1952, $25.00 minimum. The midwives recorded births in a book as a record of deliveries and for tax purposes. Licensed pattera assisted with home births on Guam until 1967, when the last midwife license expired.~~

ginen island of no birdsong

is the birth of air, is
the birth of water, is
a state between
the origin and
the end, between
birth & the beginning of
another fetid nest

—Charles Olson *from* "The Kingfishers"

~

"day seven : feather tracts visible on back, sides and head"

[we] flock to mass on sundays // grandma kneels and opens the bible as if its pages were wings \\ once i found a clutch of leathery eggs in the hollow of a fallen trunkun niyok : *coconut tree* // "more than two million brown tree snakes have been born on guam during the past 50 years" \\ avian silence // st kevin, tayuyute [ham]

~

"day ten : eyes begin to open, bill all black"

fanhasso studying the endemic marianas crow, or aga, in school // "added to the endangered species list in 1984" \\ "scientists placed electric barriers around nests, built facilities for artificial incubation, and transferred ten wild-caught crows to u.s. zoos for captive breeding" // 10,000 chamorros now live in texas \\ 7,000 in hawai'i // what does not change

~

in 2011 the last female marianas crow on guam died in captivity of kidney failure // her name was mochong \\ she was 12 years old // she leaves behind two male aga \\ one lives in captivity and the other lives in the confines of andersen air force base in northern guam

"kaaa-ah kaaa-ah"

~

"day thirteen : feathers begin breaking through skin"

fanhasso standing in line with grandma to receive the eucharist // "body of christ," the priest says, offering the host in his konnai : *hand* \\ "amen," i respond and open my påchot : *mouth* // even our tongues are 70% hånom

~

""hu hongge i lina'la'
tataotao ta'lo åmen""
i want to believe
in the resurrection of
our bodies
because [we] still feel
ghost limb pain
where our wings
once belonged

"o asaina o aniti"

#prayfor________
#prayfor________
#prayfor________
#prayfor________
#prayfor________
#prayfor________
#prayfor________
#prayfor________
#prayfor________
#prayfor________

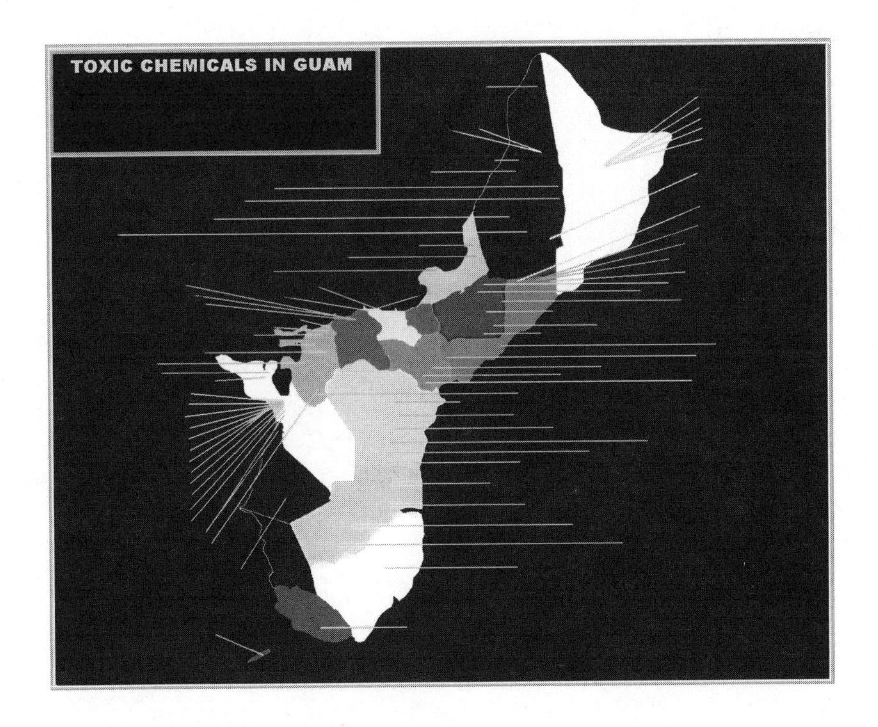

poemap based on "Toxic Chemicals of Guam: More than 100 Dumpsites with T. Chemicals, in a 30x8 Mile Island (Source: US GRAL. Accounting Office; US DoD/FUDs & the US Agency Toxic Substances, Dis.registry), Prepared by Luis Szyfres, MD, MPH--University of Guam.

its imagination

from **the legends of juan malo** *(a malologue)*

~

(the birth of Liberation Day)

I, Juan Malo, was born on July 21st, which also happens to be "Liberation Day" on Guam. This annual holiday commemorates the date in 1944 when 300 U.S. fighter jets dropped 124 tons of bombs on Guam, and thousands of American soldiers invaded our shores to "save" [us] from the Japanese. The patriotic procession takes place on Marine Corps Drive, our main highway, and includes an island-wide parade, barbecues, live hip hop, an air show, and fireworks! The invitation for Liberation Day Queen contestants has been extended to the military community. The pageant committee is looking for women ages 17 to 25 who have never been married or pregnant. The theme for the floats this year is "The Spirit of Freedom." But sadly, the governor won't allow a Texas Hold'em Poker booth. Maybe we should rename the festivities: "Limited Liberation Day." Residents can still play approved games of chance, such as enlisting in the Army, which will have an on-site recruiting booth. St. George, tayayute [ham]. My favorite part of the spectacle is when Chamorro children watch their parents stand on the sidewalk and chant, "Si Yu'us Ma'ase" : "*Thank You,*" as they bow to the soldiers marching by (many of whom are also Chamorro). Liberation Day is a must-see event for tourists, which is super awkward since most of them are Japanese. Over time, [we] have learned how to deal with this triggering trauma: don't get mad at the tourists, get them to spend their money and count it as war crimes reparations! St. Matthew, tayuyute [ham]. The outrigger canoe, Saina, first appeared in public as an entry in the 2008 parade.

This year, Chamorros will be celebrating Liberation Day in Bremerton, WA, Dayton, OH, Fort Bragg, NC, Fort Jackson, SC, Hopewell, VA, Jacksonville, FL, Killeen & Copperas Cove, TX, Port Hueneme Naval Base Ventura County, CA, San Antonio, TX, San Diego, CA, Yuba City, CA, Washington DC, and South Korea. St. Frances Xavier Cabrini, tayuyute [ham]. Despite the amount of Budweiser consumed on Liberation Day, [we] sober up after calculating the high number of sacrificial Chamorros enlisting in the U.S. military, and yet our debt to the "savior" is still ballooning out of control. Maybe next year, the theme of the parade will be: "Kao magåhet na manlibre hit? Is it true that we are liberated?"

ginen **understory**

~

(first ultrasound)

ekungok : *listen* to heartbeats
echoing // is this the sound

of our ancestors pulsing
your taut skin drum \\

pele dances towards [us]
// is our house prepared

for birth \\ the ocean absorbs
carbon dioxide then acidifies

// whales, birds, and fish
change migration patterns

\\ my mom calls from california,
talks drought and wildfires //

[neni] will be born in april
of the hottest year in history

\\ [we] buy an air conditioner,
chicken broth simmers //

"she's kicking," [you] say,
\\ i touch your warm belly

until [we] become one
body heat // "e pele ē"

(haumea)

~

out of haumea
came our apartment
in mānoa // came the empty
crib by our queen bed \\
came endless traffic
on the h-1 and likelike highways //
came nā lani ʻehā street into
kalihi valley \\ came the corner
store // came breadfruit trees
with young breadfruit \\
came coconut trees
with young coconuts // came
young islanders waiting
for the bus \\ came christian churches
and a buddhist temple // came rows
of tī plants \\ came our birthing
class at hoʻoulu ʻāina //
came chanting and mahalo
circles \\ and soon will come
24 hours of labor spiraling
out of haumea

(i tinituhon)

~

islands are beginnings

and endings

time spiral tracts

5 minutes apart

detour return

"tulu"

waves are unfolding

sentences sakman

batkon aire birthing tub

hold my shoulders

brace your hips

sounding lines measure

row distance between

breath and generations

lukao

(dear fu'una)

~

first nana,
were you pregnant
when you labored
through contracting
waves and dilating
horizons // could you
feel [us] paddling
within as you walked
to humåtak bay \\
were you scared
to give birth in this
new place // were you
worried about [us]
being safe here

**Ritidian is an ancestral Chamorro village in northern Guam. The US first classified Ritidian as a restricted military site, and then it became a wildlife preserve covering 371 acres of coral reefs and 832 acres of terrestrial habitats. Ritidian is home to the endangered Marianas fruit bat, the Mariana crow, hawksbill and green sea turtles, and many archaeological remains (inlcuding latte' stones, water wells, cave drawings, and a fishing camp). Today, the US military plans to turn Ritidian into a live firing range complex as part of the "Pacific Pivot" military buildup. "Ritidian" comes from the Chamorro word "Litekyan" which translates as to stir, or a stirring place, referring to the waters off the coast.*

(first fever)

~

[we] bring [neni] to the pediatrician // "outbreak
of enterovirus D68 in new york" \\ the nurse

recites vaccine names and expiration dates
// "outbreak of chikungunya in the caribbean,

florida, and tokelau" \\ [you] hold [neni] and sing
a mele to calm her // "outbreak of dengue fever

in china, japan, and hawai'i" \\ needle pricks,
[neni] screams // "outbreak of west nile virus

in california" \\ water-borne, insect-borne, air-
borne, food-borne // "outbreak of ebola in liberia,

sierra leone, and guinea" \\ at home we check
her temperature : 98° // "outbreak of zika virus

in brazil" \\ when the planet warms, our bodies
host fever chains of transmission // "outbreak of

measles at disneyland" \\ [we] check again : 101.6°
// no child born in this fourth era of disease

will be immune \\ her fever breaks at dawn
// please don't let our children drown in sweat

ginen **organic acts**

~

there's another story grandma carries : "once a giant guihan : *fish* began eating the center of our island" // "the men hunted, but the giant guihan hid" \\ "that's when the virgin mary came, wove her gapot ulu : *hair* into a talaya, caught the guihan, and saved [us]" // after the war (1944) (barrigada : *flank*) the united states military (tiyan : *stomach*) occupied more than half of guam (mongmong : *pulse*) including the tidelands \\ now

grandma.
barely eats.
three bites.
is full.
legs barely.
as thick.
as arms.
veins.
protrude.
from paper.
thin skin.
wings.
caught.
in talaya.
crown of.
roses.
lisayu.
rotary.
rot.

there's an older version of the story grandma never told me : once a giant guihan began eating the center of our island // the men formed a blockade with canoes and the women wove their gapot ulu into a net and chanted kantan chamorrita until the beast was lured to the surface and caught \\ [we] saved [us]

grandma forgets. how
to cook. days of the week.
my name. forgets she
no longer lives on guam.
"when are [we] going
home?" she keeps asking.

in the thirteen-month chamorro calendar, february 1st marks the new year // on that day in 2014, the cultural groups *our islands are sacred* and *hinasso* revived the lukao fuha, the annual procession to humåtak bay in honor of fu'una and puntan \\ silenced for centuries // they made offerings, asked for blessings \\ "hinasso" translates as *imagination*, *thought*, *memory*, or *reflection* // the people wore åtte'long : *black*, å'paka : *white*, and agaga': *red* clothes \\ the same colors [we] painted our canoes

"manhihigai hit pa'go"
(even our hair is 10% hånom)
"para ta afte in gima'-ta"
"para i leheng-ta para u fa'maolek" :
          "*for the care of our shelter*"
"para todu i familia-ta"

ginen **Ka Lāhui o ka Pō Interview**

September 27, 2014

~

[me]: I started packing for the hospital and going over the route in my mind. She didn't talk much. She wanted me to hold her. It was a long time of just being quiet. I was massaging her, taking showers with her, feeding her.

Helen: Marla was born in the early morning, 1982. I was a legal secretary during the day and transcribing at night. When the contractions came they were sharp, and we went to Guam Memorial Hospital. It was midnight and the midwife was with me.

[you]: While I was in transition I would get nauseous and throw up. So I didn't want to eat. Craig encouraged me to eat and kept bringing me food, but the only thing I could eat was pa'i'ai.

Helen: They gave me an episiotomy because Marla was big. The midwife massaged me, helped me breathe, gave me ice. I had bad back aches and when they put my legs in the stirrups, I started cramping. I felt very cold.

[me]: The hypno-birthing app described contractions as waves. Since we're islanders we related to that. So every contraction I said "ride the wave," but after 18 hours she yelled, "Stop calling them waves! They're just pain!" I didn't say a word after that.

Helen: The doctor kept telling me not to push, but I couldn't hold it and ended up pushing sooner than I should have. Then I tore. I could feel the blood coming out of my body. They had a pot at the end of the delivery table and I could hear the blood flowing into the pot.

[me]: When an intense contraction came, it was like she went to this deep place. She called me, but she wasn't looking at me. She was looking at someone else. She was talking to baby, and I think she was talking to her dad.

Helen: It was then I saw a light, like a tunnel. I felt outside my body. I was looking at myself thinking, I'm gonna die. And then the doctor was screaming at your dad to get out of the room. I remember that white light.

[you]: I was talking to my dad, who passed away when I was eleven. I felt like I was in a different space, here but not here. I kept thinking about people who I had lost, and I felt them around me. I could talk with them. I was also talking to baby. I was asking her to help me and telling her that it was time to come out. I was trying to prepare her.

Tom: Marla was a scary birth. The bucket, the blood. A vessel burst. A hemorrhage. Your mom turned white. The doctor yelled, and they pushed me out of the room. I stood outside the door, looking through. Finally the bleeding stopped. I remember Marla had a lot of hair.

~~"Despite the nurse-midwives' creditable record of services, their role in assisting with home births in Guam has disappeared, owing to a combination of factors such as development of the U.S. medical care model, the end of midwifery training, new licensure requirements, increased numbers of physicians, and the opening of new hospital facilities. The focus on the birthing process shifted away from families and home to an institutionalized medical setting." —Karen A. Cruz~~
~~*from The Pattera of Guam: Their Story and Legacy*~~

ginen island of no birdsong

~

"day nineteen : breast feathers breaking from sheaths"

fanhasso the fighter jets breaking the sky above the halom tano' : *deep jungle* behind grandma's house // native birds once ate insects and wove nests from spider webs \\ "guam now has forty times more spiders than other nearby islands"

~

i was 20 years old the first time i saw a living micronesian kingfisher // the shy bird hid in the corner of the hi-tech cage at the san diego zoo \\ "view inside a micronesian kingfisher nest log through live video feed" // it didn't make a sound \\ "meet siheky! the new mascot for the pacific islands club resort in tumon, guam!" // st anthony of padua, tayuyute [ham]

~

"day twenty : skin completely covered by pin feathers"

"On January 1, 2014, the Smithsonian National Zoo rung in the New Year with the hatching of a Micronesian kingfisher, the most endangered species in its collection. The animal care staff is hand-raising the chick, which involves feeding it at two-hour intervals, seven to eight times per day. This birth brings the total population to 129 birds, all of which live in captivity" // 70,000 chamorros still live on guam \\ 150,000 now live off-island // is migration our "species survival plan" "kshh-skshh-skshh-kroo-ee, kroo-ee, kroo-ee"

~

when [we] return to the pew after communion, i count how many people are standing in line to receive the eucharist // whose bodies are given, whose bodies are taken \\ "let go, let go, let go," said the last marianas crow, "human kind can't bear very much diversity"

"kaaa-ah kaaa-ah"

~

""hu hongge i lina'la'
tataotao ta'lo åmen""
i believe in the resilience
of our bodies
because our hearts
are 75% hånom
and every pulse is
i napu : *a wave*
accustomed
to breaking

"o asaina o aniti o asaina o aniti"

#prayfor________
#prayfor________
#prayfor________
#prayfor________
#prayfor________
#prayfor________
#prayfor________
#prayfor________
#prayfor________
#prayfor________

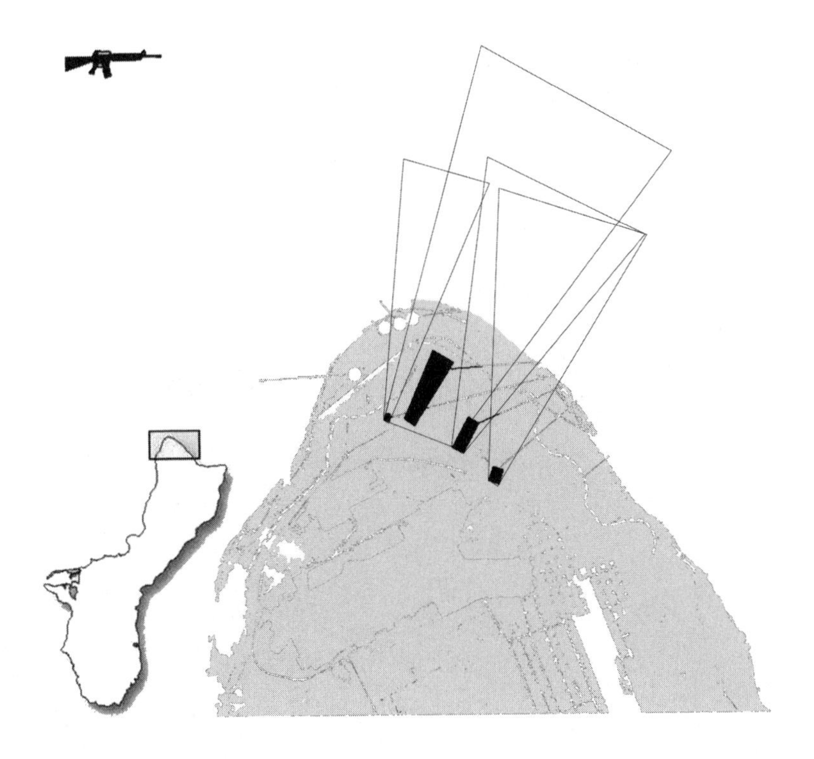

poemap based on the “How Ritidian may be affected” map, illustrated by Cid Caser/Pacific Daily News, Source Draft Environmental Impact Statement, April 2014. The map includes the text: “The new preferred site for the Marine Corps’ Live Fire Training Range Complex, at Northwest Field, which is part of Andersen Air Force Base, is shown. Use of the site could limit public access to Ritidian beach, caves and hiking trails.” The black areas represent the proposed firing range area, the space projecting from those areas represent the munitions zone, which will impact the Guam National Wildlife Refuge at Ritidian.

people around the world

from **the legends of juan malo** *(a malologue)*

~

(the birth of SPAM)

SPAM was born on July 5, 1937, in Austin, Minnesota, the home of Hormel (pronounced "Hor-mal," like "Nor-mal"). Eight pounds of SPAM die in a Chamorro stomach each year, which is more per capita than any other ethno-intestinal tract in the world. Guam is an acronym for "Give Us American Meat." Our guttural love of SPAM was born in 1944, when the shiny cans were berthed from aircraft carriers. This fateful day is commemorated as "The Feast Day of the Immaculate Consumption." St. Anthony the Abbot, tayayute [ham]. The rest of the story is digestional genealogy, a delicious cycle. Sadly, military recruiters are now worried that young Chamorros have become too obese to enlist in the armed forces. "Guam is Where America's Impure Pork Products End!" At this year's SPAM Cook-Off in Guam, my uncle's "Pika Spam Pierogi" ousted my auntie's "Crispy Wanton Spam Ravioli" for first place. He won a free roundtrip ticket to the 14,000 square foot SPAM museum in Minnesota #cubistartyoucaneat. Turkey SPAM, hot and spicy SPAM, garlic SPAM, SPAM lite, Portuguese Sausage flavored SPAM, etc. WSFWJE? (What SPAM Flavor Would Jesus Eat?). My food philosophy is simple: I eat therefore I SPAM. The name itself stands for : Specially Processed Army Meal, Sacred Pork And Medicine, Super Pink Artificial Meat, Snake Pigeon And Mongoose, or Some Pigs Are Missing. At the SPAM factory, nearly 20,000 hogs are slaughtered every day. More than 1,000 severed pig heads slide down the conveyor belt every hour. Undocumented migrants slice ears, clip snouts, chisel cheeks, scoop eyes, carve tongues, and scrape mouths #everythingbutthesqueal. Every three seconds, a compressed-air hose blasts pig brains from a denuded skull into a barrel. Rosy mist, strawberry milkshake, Pepto-Bismol. Google: "the SPAM factory's dirty little secret." St. Bonaventura, tayuyute [ham]. "Oh baby, here I am, come rub up on my belly like SPAM jelly / Oh baby, here I am, come rub up on my belly like SPAM jelly / Spam-Spam-Jelly / Spam-Spam Jelly!" #mandatorymarley. My favorite scene in John Steinbeck's *The Grapes of Wrath* (b. 1939) is when the tractor driver is on lunch break near a tenant house eating a SPAM sandwich. The curious, starving children surround him like a dust storm. Once upon spiral time, a Chamorro brother and sister refused to eat SPAM, so their Authentic Chamorro Grandmother banished them from Guam and cursed them to a life as diasporic vegetarians. St. David, tayuyute [ham]. The siblings migrated to Minnesota, where they opened the world's first "vegan butcher shop" and sold meatless meats at farmers markets and pop-up culinary events. They dream of creating the perfect vegan SPAM. They try combinations of vital wheat gluten, garbanzo beans, tapioca flour, peanut butter, and spices. "The flavor's good but the texture's off," they say in unison. "SPAM is just a difficult whale to catch." If they ever succeed, I will never eat it #burp.

ginen **understory**

~

(third trimester, january 27, 2014)

the wind billows our bedroom
curtains like the vowels

in *hiroshima*, *enewetak*, *mororua*
// the branches of our unborn

daughter's respiratory tree
are just beginning to radiate \\

[we] lather in coconut oil,
spoon tight like the vowels

in *nagasaki*, *trinity*, *bikini* // the sky
breaks into a thousand suns

\\ rain clouds baptize guam
in strontium-90 fallout,

circa 1954 // what cancers remain
buried in pacific bodies like unexploded

ordnances \\ what downwind toxins
will [neni] inhale when her lungs

first expand // what wars of light
will irradiate when she first opens

her sublime eyes

(papahānaumoku and wākea)

~

earth mother and sky father
embrace atop mauna kea //
then birth hoʻohokukalani,
who will birth hāloanakalaukapalili
\\ who is still, then buried, then
sprouts // in our garden,
[we] plant nine huli
from *ku maoli ola nursery* \\
the ʻoha curves towards the sky
like our daughter's spine
          in utero //
how will [we] explain to her
why the people who propose
to build a 30-meter telescope
atop this mountain yearn
to see 13 billion light years
into space, yet refuse to see
the sacredness of this place
#kūkiaʻimauna \\ look
(even our eyes are 95% hånom)
towards the center of
the pulsing heart-
shaped leaf : a single,
endless drop of

          ua

(i tinituhon)

~

wave sub traction

2 min utes apart

midwife hands push words

"fat fat"

islands are endings

and beg innings

row crown vowels

egg mucus blood bile

my first story

vocal cords umbilical chords

and your first story

ēwe apuya' *are woven* tumuge' påpa'

(even our blood is 90% hånom)

hunggan hunggan hunggan

magahet

(santa marian kamalen)
december 8th

~

during the feast day
of the immaculate conception,
the replica statue
of santa marian kamalen
is carried in procession
around hagåtña // [we] cast
rice and flowers, retelling the story :
300 years ago, a fisherman
found the statue at sea
carried by two crabs
with lit votives on their backs \\
he delivered her to a priest,
who delivered her to the governor
// today she lives in a niche
behind the altar of
the dulce nombre de maria
cathedral basilica in hagåtña \\
stolen and recovered 3 times since
// she is carved from
wood and ivory, dressed
in a pink and blue gown
with a gold crown
nesting atop her head,
from which human hair

(first birthday)

~

[you] clip her tiny fingernails // "the rape of oceania
began with guam" \\ how do [we] protect daughters

from becoming target and conquest #yesallwomen
// [you] brush her hair and sing a hawaiian nursery

rhyme about the body parts, "nā mahele o ke kino"
: "poʻo, maka, ihu, waha" (touch head, eyes, nose,

mouth) \\ who will recite the names of those
disappeared from reservations and machiladoras

#mmiw, from villages and schools #bringback
-ourgirls // "pepeiao, lima, manamanalima" (touch

ears, hold up hands, wiggle fingers) \\ [you] nurse
[neni] and fall asleep, still latched // "kuli, wāwae,

"manamanawāwae" (touch knees, feet, wiggle toes)
// for a moment, she smiles // "me kuʻu poʻohiwi"

(rest hands on shoulders) \\ what does she dream
\\ i whisper : "[neni], no matter how far from home

the storms take you, remember to carry our words
in your canoe // [neni], remember : you will always

belong, you will always be sheltered, and you
will always be sacred in our ocean of stories

ginen **organic acts**

"The journey commences with a star falling from the sky to signify a birth and is represented by the slightly turned up bow of a canoe. The journey continues throughout life, much like the narrow hull of a canoe. Finally, the journey concludes upon the death of an individual when one's spirit travels upward along the turned-up stern of a canoe and returns as a star that is recovered into the sky."

—Maria Yatar *from* "Navigating Modernity"

~

in 2010, i bring copies of my new book *[saina]* to my parents' house // mom exclaims to grandma : "look, it's your story, you're famous now" \\ i don't have the heart to tell them that no one reads poetry

mom and auntie take turns reading aloud to grandma
in the living room // when the first section ends, auntie
asks : "what happens next, is that the end" \\ they turn the
pages until they reach the next excerpt // "here, the
organic acts continue"

grandma keeps a copy of my book on her bedside table next to her altar // she feels scared at night because she doesn't remember where she lives \\ mom reminds her : "you live in california now, with me, your eldest daughter" // she reads her the poem for comfort

~

my wife, daughter, and i travel to california for the first time
in the summer of 2015, which was the warmest in history //
grandma asks : "who

are you?" "i'm craig,
helen's son" "do you live
in guam?" "no, grandma,
i live in hawai'i" "oh i love
hawai'i, the weather
is just like guam"
[neni]

walks to her, opens her arms // grandma kisses her cheek,
breathes deep her baby scent \\ lukao between four generations
// even our skin is 40% hånom

~

grandma says : "I really miss my mom. her voice is like my
voice. when I say rosary I can still hear her, even here in
california" (even here) // [we] pray : "santa maria nanan yu'us,
tayayute ham, ni i manisao pago yan i oran finatai-mami åmen"

~

during seasonal fish runs, chamorros hemmed
"manhihigai hit pa'go"
the tidelands to cast talaya, cook, and share food
"para ta afte in gima'-ta"
for miles and hours kantan chamorrita
"para I leheng-ta para u fa'maolek"
was chanted in echo location
"para todu i familia-ta" : *for all of our family*

ginen **Ka Lāhui o ka Pō Interview**

(September 27, 2014)

~

[me]: She labored first in the tub, then on the bed. I tried to be calm and strong for her. Her legs were shaking (even our muscles are 75% hånom)

Helen: The doctor and midwife were stuffing pads in me to stop the hemorrhaging and bleeding. My body was shaking like I was having a seizure. I really thought I was going to die. And I felt so cold. They kept wrapping me with blankets. I just kept praying, "don't let me die."

[you]: I pulled my knee to my shoulders. I didn't know I could do that. It was uncomfortable, but it worked. During the pushing, I remember Craig at my side.

Helen: After awhile the bleeding stopped. Marla was okay, just a little jaundice. They took me to another room at the end of the hall, and it was right next to where they kept the convicts. So your dad stayed to guard the door.

[me]: I was in awe. She went into mana wahine mode. When she was pushing, she was so strong and powerful. The crown of baby's head came out a little then it went back in. This happened several times. Then with the next push the whole head came out and I was like "OMG her head's so big"! Then her body came out and I was like "OMG" then she opened her eyes and I was "OMG"!

[you]: (to [neni]) Yes, you looked at daddy when you came out. (to Craig) Good thing you didn't drop her.

[me]: Yeah she was so slippery when she came out, so I pushed her onto her chest. Then the blood came.

[you]: They had to give me a shot of pitocin afterward to stop the blood. I tore a little bit, but I didn't need stitches. Then they gave me salt water to drink.

Helen: When the nurse brought Marla in, I was so weak because the blood loss. They gave me the baby to hold. I tried to hold the baby but I fainted and fell to the floor.

[me]: This birthing class was empowering. It gave us a place to talk about what we were going through. It gave [you] space to cry and be with other Hawaiians who had the same fears. They reminded us that our people have given birth for thousands of years. Without the class, we wouldn't have had the courage to give birth at home.

Helen: They gave me some kind of shot to stop the bleeding, maybe pitocin. They kept me in the hospital for a couple of days, but I couldn't sleep. I kept praying, "dear god please don't let me die." When they finally let me go home, I could not believe that Marla had so much hair.

[neni]: (gurgling/baby talk). **[me]:** (Speaking for daughter) "Now, let me tell you what really happened" (laughter)

~~U.S. Naval orders mandated that the placenta and umbilical cord must be burned because they were considered hazardous waste.~~ Defying these orders, the pattera continued to help families bury the placenta in the land under or near the house (in our freezer, there is a plastic ziplock bag marked "placenta." Someday we will bury it at your grandparents house in Kula, Maui, on the slopes of Haleakalā). #placentalpolitics

ginen island of no birdsong

No story or song will translate the full impact of falling, or the inverse power of rising up. Of rising up.

—Joy Harjo *from* "A Postcolonial Tale"

~

"day twenty-seven : feathers emerge from sheaths"

[we] flock to recruitment centers, ensnared // *a cage can be either solid material wire mesh or* ... \\ "chamorros have the highest per capita enlistment rates in the united states" // is this our species survival plan

"day twenty-nine : perching"

birds once digested, husked, and scattered seeds // "caught in the web of extinction, the native fire tree, or hayun lågu, was added to the endangered species list in 1987" \\ trophic cascade, descending plumeria, colony collapse // "guam is such a fascinating natural laboratory, we have so many questions!" // st dorothy, tayuyute [ham]

~

"The 36th Civil Engineer Squadron Environmental Flight hosted a volunteer workday for military personnel and their families by assisting in the replacement and repair of a seven-foot-high fence around the endangered fire tree on Andersen Air Force Base...The fire tree is the last of its kind on Guam. More than 40 volunteers showed up, with representatives from 36th CES, 734th Air

Mobility Squadron, 36th Mobility Response Squadron, Naval Airborne Weapons Maintenance Unit 1, U.S. Fish and Wildlife Service, and Guam Division of Aquatic and Wildlife Resources. The workday was set up...to increase the ties between natural resources management and military readiness." (2012)

~

"day thirty : fully feathered"

fanhasso grandma gave me her rosary at the guam plasan batkon aire : *airport* // i clutched the beads while standing in line at the boarding gate \\ home is an archipelago

of prayer

~

"day thirty-five : fledging"

""hu hongge i lina'la'
tataotao ta'lo åmen""
i believe in the resurgence
of our bodies because
[we] are the seeds
ginen the last hayun lågu
waiting to be rooted
into kantan chamorrita,
waiting to be raised
once more into lukao

"kaaa-ah o asaina kaaa-ah o aniti"
"kshh-skshh-skshh-kroo-ee o asaina
kroo-ee kroo-ee o aniti"

#prayfor________
#prayfor________
#prayfor________
#prayfor________
#prayfor________
#prayfor________
#prayfor________
#prayfor________
#prayfor________
#prayfor________

are dying

ginen **Mahalo Circle, 2013-2015** (*for Brandy*)

~

"But islands can only exist
if we have loved in them."

—Derek Walcott *from* "Islands"

~

Mahalo Kalihi Valley, the Ko'olau mountains, and the island of
O'ahu

Mahalo *Kōkua Kalihi Valley Comprehensive Family Services* for
being non-profit and birthing *Ho'oulu 'Āina*, 100 acres leased
from the state park, whose name translates as *to grow the land and
to grow because of the land* // Mahalo volunteers who removed
the invasive albizia so light could heal the native flora \\ Mahalo
for planting a community garden and for not spraying pesticides
// Mahalo Puni and auntie Ka'iulani for starting each Hawaiian
birthing class with a chant honoring the valley, and a mahalo circle
honoring those [we] are grateful for \\ Mahalo for serving dinner
of local 'uala and poi, garden salad, and organic chicken soup //
Mahalo for brewing 'ōlena and māmaki tea on those cool rainy
nights

Mahalo akua for blessing us with ua : *rain* when [we] visited
the 4-acre family-owned *Kūpa'a Farm*, whose name translates as
steadfast and *faithful*, on the slopes of Haleakalā, Maui, in 2013
// Mahalo Janet and Gerry for not spraying pesticides \\ Mahalo
for using cover crops and perennial vegetative barriers // Mahalo
for growing coffee trees under the shade of koa and monkeypod \\

Mahalo for letting us smell the compost // Mahalo for harvesting 50 pounds of beets, eggplant, carrots, lettuce, kale, papaya, lilikoi, and coffee beans for the wedding

Mahalo *Mana Foods* in Pāʻia, Maui, for sourcing local ʻuala, ʻōlena, ginger, pineapple, dragon fruit, mango, sweet onion, banana, macadamia nuts, and lychee // Mahalo for giving your compostable byproducts to local farms

Mahalo *Kula Country Farms* for the strawberries // i hope to bring my daughter to the You-Pick patch someday

Mahalo hippies with blond dreadlocks for selling unhusked coconuts from the bed of your pickup truck at the *Upcountry Farmers' Market*

Mahalo *Pukalani Superette* for sourcing a local 10-pound rib eye roast for me from *Maui Cattle Company* // Mahalo *Maui Cattle Company* for feeding your animals grass

Mahalo *Whole Foods* in Kahului, Maui, for sourcing a local 10-pound mahimahi for me // Mahalo to the cashier who only charged me $30 for the whole fish, an unexpected wedding gift

Mahalo *Costco* in Kahului for the 10 pounds of imported, organic chicken thighs // why is it so hard to source local chicken here when they run wild everywhere

Mahalo *Tamura's Fine Wine & Liquors* in Kahului for sourcing local beer // Mahalo *Maui Brewing Company* for your *Bikini Blonde Lager*, *CocoNut Porter*, and *Big Swell IPA* \\ Mahalo for giving your spent grain to local farmers for feed and compost // St. Heineken, please forgive our trespasses

Mahalo *Madre Chocolate* for being bean to bar // Mahalo for the Farm to Factory Tour, for letting us pick cacao from the *Reppun Farm* in Waiāhole, O'ahu, and taste fresh cacao pulp \\ Mahalo to the Reppun family for struggling for land and water rights decades ago

Mahalo *Maui Bees* in Kula for raw wildflower honey and for not treating the bees with chemicals

Mahalo *Stillwell's Bakery* in Wailuku, Maui, for the three layer wedding cake hand-delivered to Huelo // Mahalo each layer of lilikoi cream, coconut cream, and custard cream, I love you all equally, as if you were my own future children \\ Mahalo Brandy for decorating the cake with pink anthuriums & purple orchids from your grandparents' garden in Kula

Mahalo family-run *Noho'ana Farm*, whose name translates as *lifestyle*, for restoring 2 acres of land and 500 year old lo'i in Waikapū, Maui // Mahalo Hōkūao for making 10 pounds of fresh poi on the day of the wedding \\ Mahalo *Hui o Nā Wai 'Ehā* for struggling for water rights in East Maui, where the *Wailuku Sugar Company* has diverted, for more than a century, the "Four Great Waters": Waihe'e River, Waiehu Stream, Wailuku River, and Waikapū Stream

Mahalo La'akea for sourcing 3 pounds of handcrafted *Puna Pa'akai* sea salt from the Big Island and mailing it to me in Maui // it blessed the food and the venue

Mahalo Calrose white rice, imported from California, for filling our plates // Mahalo *Mama Sita achiote powder*, imported from the Philippines, for transforming the white rice into a thousand tiny red rose petals \\ Calrose is Calrose is Calrose is Calrose
Mahalo Lauralei, my mother-in-law, for making the local pohole

salad // Mahalo for asking your friend, whom I call uncle, for sourcing the local ahi limu poke \\ Mahalo cousins, Taylor and Ala, for peeling and chopping fruits and vegetables // Mahalo Brian, my brother, for grilling the chicken, roasting the rib eye, and being my best man \\ Mahalo ninu and nina for flying from Guam to Maui, and for grilling the fish and making the kelaguen // Mahalo, auntie Cat, for chopping the chicken for the kelaguen \\ Mahalo uncle Dave for not drinking all the beers // Mahalo Grandma Kekauoha for toasting with your glass of champagne \\ Mahalo my brothers-in-law, Justin and Kyle, for husking the coconuts // Mahalo Roanne, my cousin, for grating the coconuts for the kelaguen \\ Mahalo Marla, my sister, for being a bridesmaid, and for making the coconut milk // Mahalo Janelle, my sister-in-law, for hand mixing the Waikapū poi with water while you were 7 months pregnant // Mahalo Ku'i and Hālona for setting the tables \\ Mahalo Kawaianu for being the flower girl // Mahalo Georganne and Herve for your friendship and helping hands // Mahalo Grandpa Kekauoha for blessing the meal \\ Mahalo, mom and dad, for always feeding me // Mahalo for being brave enough to migrate across the ocean, for building a new home for [us], and for teaching me how to navigate this world \\ I will always carry your stories with me // Mahalo to all our family who traveled to the wedding and served our guests dinner \\ Mahalo to all our guests for your gifts and the gift of your presence // Mahalo, dear readers, for joining [us] at the table of this poem, please eat until you're full, there's more than enough for everyone, and please don't leave until [we] give you a full plate to take home for your meal tomorrow

Mahalo Brandy for saying ʻae : *yes*, which sounds similar to the Hawaiian words ʻai : to eat and ai : to make love #sexualkaona

Mahalo *Mānoa Community Garden Association* for giving me a plot after 9 months on the waiting list // Mahalo for banning pesticides in the garden \\ Mahalo invasive California nut grass for teaching me insistence // Mahalo *City Mill* for sourcing seedlings and tools (I don't forgive you for stocking shelves of Roundup) \\ Mahalo *Whole Foods* in Kahala, O'ahu, for sourcing imported organic seeds // Mahalo *College of Tropical Agriculture and Human Resources* at the University of Hawai'i, Mānoa (UHM) for sourcing local seeds \\ Mahalo *Hui Kū Maoli Ola* in He'eia, O'ahu, for being the world's largest native Hawaiian plant nursery and for sourcing different varieties of kalo, which Brandy and I planted in the garden // Mahalo communal water hose \\ Mahalo Mānoa rain water

Mahalo *My Pregnancy* app for comparing week-by-week fetal growth to poppy seed, sesame seed, lentil, blueberry, kidney bean, grape, kumquat, fig, lime, pea, lemon, apple, avocado, turnip, tomato, banana, carrot, mango, corn, rutabaga, scallion, cauliflower, eggplant, squash, cabbage, coconut, jicama, pineapple, cantaloupe, romaine lettuce, swiss chard, leek, watermelon, pumpkin // What if I coded a Pacific version of this app: white sugar, pa'akai, achiote seed, boiled peanut, crackseed, coffee bean, macnut, Li Hing Mui, dohne', vienna sausage, calamansi, guava, lilikoi, mountain apple, avocado, can of tuna, tabasco, banana, heineken, mango, can of corned beef, kalo, spam musubi, 2 scoops white rice, shoyu bottle, non-gmo papaya, turkey tail, coconut, ahi poke bowl, pineapple, zip pac, plate lunch, ulu, costo mayonaisse jar, and ipu

Mahalo *Kōkua Market* for being Honolulu's only co-op grocery // Mahalo for sourcing local vegetable and meats \\ Mahalo Lynette for allowing me to host a poetry reading at the store // Mahalo to my students for reciting their food poetry in the produce section

Mahalo *Down to Earth* for being Honolulu's only vegetarian grocery store // Mahalo for your healthy and bright salad bar, which makes Brandy smile as wide as her growing belly

Mahalo Kapiʻolani Community College Farmers' Market // I'm sorry we stopped visiting but you have become an overcrowded tourist attraction

Mahalo 23-acre *Maʻo Organic Farms* in Waiʻanae, Oʻahu, for birthing a mala ʻai ʻopio : *youth food garden* // Mahalo for your yellow Community Supported Agriculture (CSA) box, with the slogan "No Panic Go Organic" in green lettering, which I pick up every week from the Urban and Regional Planning building on the UHM campus

Mahalo UHM for giving me a job teaching poetry so that I can afford to buy local foods // yet why are they more expensive than food imported from thousands of miles away

Mahalo to my homemade, no-waste, 100% local smoothie, which I've affectionately named, "The Green Island," whose recipe took me months to perfect: banana, non-gmo papaya, pineapple, ginger, ʻōlena, kale, lime, and filtered tap water // St. Vitamix, puree for [us]

Mahalo *Student Organic Farm Training* (S.O.F.T.) in Mānoa, for letting me drop off my vegetable waste into your compost pile // Mahalo mythic albino cockroach for saying hello as I turned the compost

Mahalo clean tap water and Brita pitcher // Mahalo all the "embedded water" used to grow our food

Mahalo *Hawaiʻi Food Bank* for stocking enough to feed the population for seven days if the container ships stop coming // Mahalo to the long-time employee who trained me to sort produce donations \\ Mahalo *Costco* for donating hundreds of bananas from Ecuador, clementines from Chile, oranges from Australia, and cabbage from Mexico // Mahalo *Aloun Farms* for donating thousands of local green bell peppers, therefore never ask for whom the bell pepper rots, it rots for thee \\ Mahalo nameless farm in Watsonville, California, for donating thousands of strawberries, some of which are covered in white mold // Mahalo nameless farm in Santa Cruz, California, for donating hundreds of lettuce heads, whose brown layers peel away easily : lettuce pray and make our salvage \\ Mahalo cases of "mainland shell protected" eggs donated from California, Arizona, and Washington, stamped "US" and still cold from the chill // Mahalo early morning radio DJs for always playing Bob Marley because "there ain't no hiding place from the Father of Creation" \\ Mahalo baby flies, fat flies, and dead flies for teaching me how time flies when you volunteer // Mahalo mop bucket for squeezing the dirty water after I mop the grime \\ Mahalo Mothers of Slow Rot, Mothers of the Still Edible, Mothers of Soup Kitchens, Mothers of Food Pantries, Mothers of Leftovers, Mothers of Canned Goods, pray for [us]

Mahalo auntie Kaiulani for organizing the monthly *Decolonize Your Diet* series at *Roots Café* in *Kokua Kalihi Valley* // Mahalo Aiko and Kelsey for making homemade, locally sourced SPAM for "De-processing Spam" night \\ Mahalo for inviting me to deliver my talk, "Uncle Spam Wants You," about the gastro-colonial and military history of my favorite canned meat // Mahalo Brandy for performing my poem, "Spam's Carbon Footprint," with me, you are the Spam jelly to my lucky belly

Mahalo Hanale and Meghan of *Homestead Poi* for your kalo farm in Waiāhole // Mahalo for not spraying pesticides \\ Mahalo for allowing my Pacific poetry class to visit // Mahalo for delivering your poi to *Kokua Market*, which I bought every week during Brandy's pregnancy, and which was the first solid food (mixed with breastmilk) [we] fed our daughter

Mahalo *Mana Ai* in Kaneohe, O'ahu, for paying kalo farmers fair wages, for cooking and pounding kalo into pa'i'ai // Mahalo for selling the pa'i'ai in tī leaves as opposed to plastic \\ Mahalo to all the activists and farmers who fought to legalize pa'i'ai // Mahalo to the activists who stopped UHM scientists from genetically engineering and patenting kalo

Mahalo Papahānaumoku and Wākea for birthing Ho'ohokukalani, who gave birth to the stars and to Hāloanakalaukapalili, whose name translates as *the long stem whose leaves tremble in the wind,* who was stillborn then buried, and from whose grave grew the first kalo // Mahalo elder brother for feeding us

Mahalo saina and kūpuna for carefully packing the kalo, niyok, lemmai, 'uala, 'ōlena, and mai'a into your sakman and wa'a (what war, what disease, what disaster were you migrating from) // Mahalo for reading the stars as if they were maps constellating a story of new beginnings \\ Mahalo for dreaming an island for [us] // Mahalo for loving these islands, for planting crops and creation stories

Mahalo, creation stories, for surviving // Mahalo for hiding in that place in our bodies that no one can convert or steal or behead or ban or bury or burn or shoot or shackle or colonize \\ Mahalo for carrying the weight of our origins in the hull of your memories and in the rope of your words // Mahalo for navigating all these distances and all these generations \\ Mahalo for reminding [us] who [we] are and where [we] come from // Mahalo for giving us the strength to say : no, [we] won't let them define [us], no, we won't let them confine [us], no, [we] won't let them silence [us]

Mahalo saina and kūpuna for planting as many trees as you could while everyone around you was dying // Mahalo for digging as many gardens and lo'i as you could while everyone around you was dying \\ Mahalo for saving as many seeds as you could while everyone around you was dying // Mahalo for passing down as many stories as you could while everyone around you was dying \\ Mahalo for giving [us] the strength to say : no, [we] won't let them poison our land and water anymore, no, [we] won't let them say our homes are wastelands or idle assets or military bases // [we] promise to protect and defend our sacred islands

Mahalo saina and kūpuna for eating canned goods, flap meats, and processed foods to survive // Mahalo for cooking foreign ingredients in recipes that taste like home \\ Mahalo for feeding [us] what you could afford // Mahalo for carrying the burden of disease so maybe we wouldn't have to // Mahalo for giving [us] the strength to say : no, [we] won't let them force feed [us] anymore

Mahalo Hawai'i nei for nurturing me even though I'm not from here // Mahalo for teaching me aloha 'āina \\ Mahalo for this dream of my daughter volunteering in the lo'i, dancing with our saina and kūpuna, dancing with our wind and tree relatives, dancing with our water and dirt relatives, dancing with our fish and bird relatives, dancing with our fruit and vegetable relatives, dancing with our more-than-human family of abundance

Mahalo Brandy for loving and caring for me // Mahalo for birthing and breastfeeding [neni] \\ Mahalo for gifting me this dream of 'ohana, this dream of belonging, this dream of our daughter, barefoot and dancing, her hair cascading into the past and braiding future generations // hu *i* guaiya hao, hu guaiya *love* hao, hu guaiya hao *[you]* \\ *mahalo hånom mahalo håga mahalo hånom*

#prayfor________
#prayfor________
#prayfor________
#prayfor________
#prayfor________
#prayfor________
#prayfor________
#prayfor________
#prayfor________
#prayfor________

ginen **sourcings**

for notes, sources, citations, and further material and context for the poems in this book, please visit

omnidawn.com/sources-from-unincorporated-territory-lukao/

Acknowledgements

thanks to all the editors of the following anthologies and literary journals that published versions of the poems in this book:

Poetry Magazine, *The Academy of American Poets*, *Split This Rock*, *New American Writing*, *The Colorado Review*, *The Berkeley Poetry Review*, *The Hawai'i Review*, *Dusie Literary Journal*, *The Capilano Literary Review*, *The Cordite Review*, *Plume Review*, *Columbia College Chicago Review*, *Matter: A Literary Journal of Political Poetry*, *Shake the Tree Poetry Anthology*, *Local Voices: An Anthology*, and *Indigenous Writers from Micronesia Anthology*.

thanks to the founders of omnidawn publishing, rusty and ken, for all your support and guidance over the years. thank you for continuing to launch this project into the world. thank you, rusty, for your generous editorial feedback, you are such an incredible teacher.

saina ma'ase to my mom and dad, this work would not be possible without your endless love. saina ma'ase to my brother and sister for all your support.

mahalo nui to brandy, my wife and partner, for inspiring me with all the beautiful things you do. none of these poems would be possible without you. mahalo nui to my daughter, kaikainali'i, for giving me hope for the future.

photo credit: Hannah Ensor

Dr. Craig Santos Perez is a native Chamorro from the Pacific Island of Guåhan (Guam). He holds an MFA in Creative Writing from the University of San Francisco and a PhD in Ethnic Studies from the University of California, Berkeley. He has has received fellowships from the Ford Foundation and the Lannan Foundation. He works as an Associate Professor in the English Department, and as an Affiliate Faculty with the Center for Pacific Islands Studies and the Indigenous Politics Program, at the University of Hawaiʻi, Mānoa.

Craig authored three previous poetry books, *from unincorporated territory [hacha]* (2008), *from unincorporated territory [saina]* (2010, a finalist for the Los Angeles Times Book Prize and a winner of the PEN Center USA/Poetry Society of America Literary Prize), and *from unincorporated territory [guma']* (2014, winner of the American Book Award). Craig has co-edited three anthologies: *Chamorro Childhood* (2009), *Home Islands: New Writing from Guam & Hawaii* (2017), and *Pacific Literature and the Environment* (forthcoming). He is the co-founder of Ala Press, and an editorial board member of Sun Tracks (University of Arizona Press) and *The Contemporary Pacific*. He edited the "New Pacific Islander Poetry" folio in *Poetry Magazine* (2016).

In 2010, the Guam Legislature recognized Craig "as an accomplished poet who has been a phenomenal ambassador for our island, eloquently conveying through his words, the beauty and love that is the Chamorro culture."

Website: www.craigsantosperez.com

from unincorporated territory [lukao]
by Craig Santos Perez

Cover art:
Photograph by Jack Gray,"The Matao New Performance Project
at Lasso' Fuha developing Fanhasso, a contemporary dance directed by
Dåkot-ta Alcantara-Camacho at the Festival of Pacific Arts 2016"
Photograph by Craig Santos Perez, "Kaikainali'i at the Honolulu Aquarium"

"poemaps" (poem-maps) designed by Craig Santos Perez & Donovan Kūhiō Colleps;
created by Donovan Kūhiō Colleps.

Cover typeface: Palatino LT Std & Perpetua Std
Interior typefaces: Adobe Garamond Pro

Cover & Interior layout by Cassandra Smith
Design by Craig Santos Perez

Offset printed in the United States
by Edwards Brothers Malloy, Ann Arbor, Michigan
On 55# Glatfelter B18 Antique
Acid Free Archival Quality Recycled Paper

Publication of this book was made possible in part by gifts from:
The Clorox Company
The New Place Fund
Robin & Curt Caton

Omnidawn Publishing
Oakland, California
2017